How We Move! Book 1 in the Young Athletic Movement Series
written by Ray Terry
Technical Consultant: Erwin Seguia PT, DPT, SCS, CSCS
Published by Young Athletic Movement Severna Park, MD
21146
© 2018 -2023 YAM, LLC
All rights reserved. No portion of this book may be reproduced in any form without permission from the publisher, except as permitted by U.S. copyright law. For permissions contact: rayjr@imandcd.com

1st
Edition

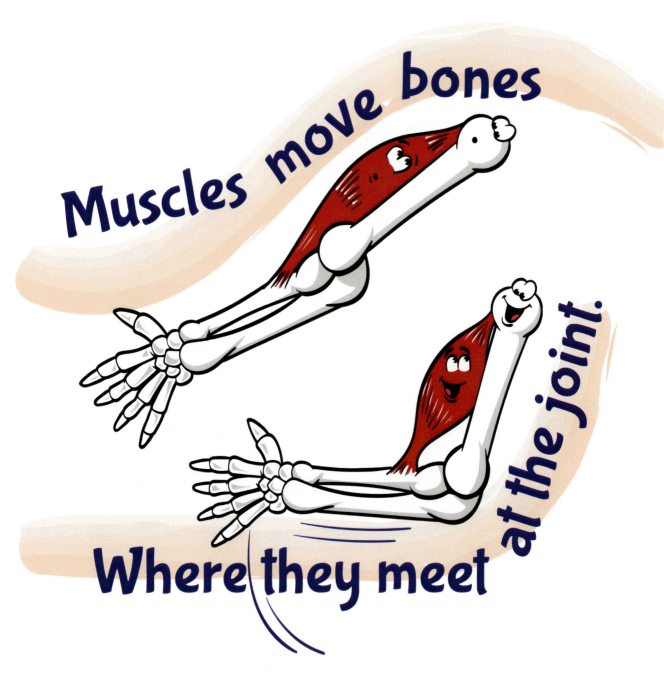

# We breathe in for

# and breathe out for

# Next in a seat we will properly sit

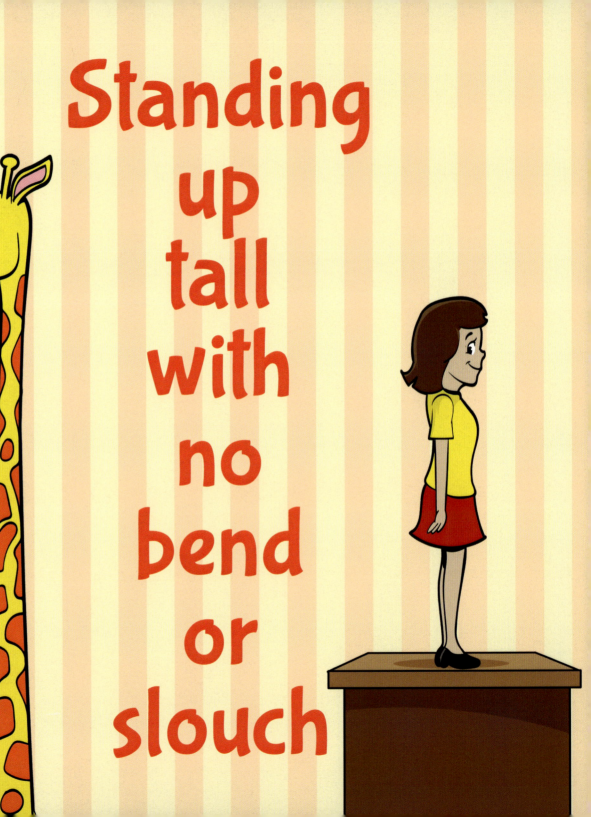

Next walking with PURPOSE.
Hold your head nice and HIGH